Everton
1878
NIL SATIS NISI OPTIMUM

THE OFFICIAL
EVERTON
ANNUAL 2026

Written by Darren Griffiths
Designed by Lucy Boyd

g

A Grange Publication

© 2025. Published by Grange Communications Ltd., Edinburgh, under licence from Everton Football Club.

Grange Communications Ltd., 25 Herbert Place, Dublin, D02 AY86 frontdesk@grangecommunications.co.uk

Printed in Romania.

Photographs © Everton Football Club

ISBN 978 1 917538 40 4

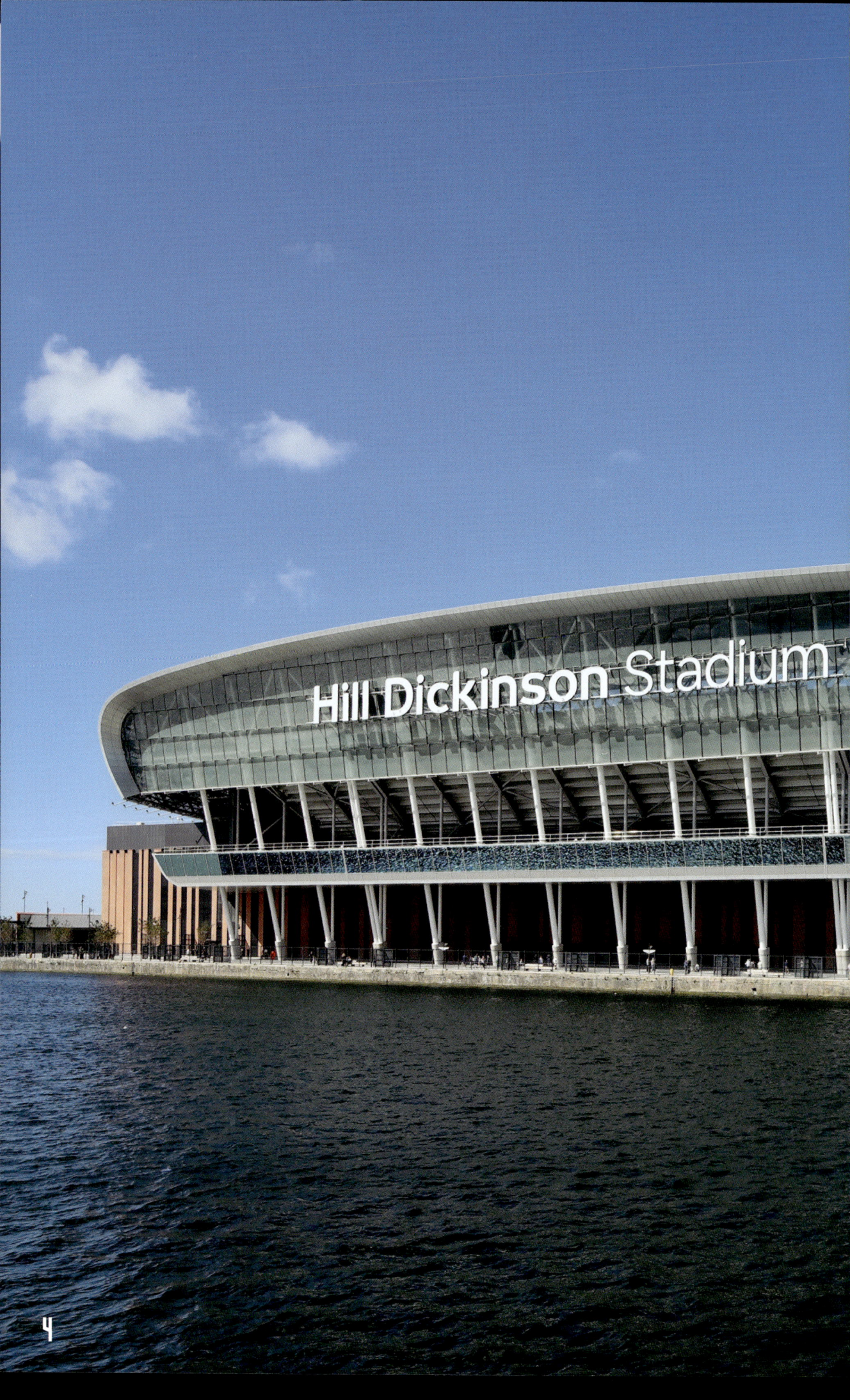

CONTENTS

DAVID MOYES

During the summer of 2025, David Moyes was acknowledged by the League Managers Association (LMA) for reaching one thousand matches as a manager.

It's a testament to the longevity of a career in what can be the most precarious of positions.

Moyes started life in the dug-out as the Player/Manager of Preston North End in 1998. His impact at Deepdale was immense. He won promotion from the third tier in 2000 and almost got the Lancashire outfit into the Premier League—losing in the play-off final at Wembley in 2001.

He stayed in the hot-seat after finally hanging his boots up and the bigger clubs began to take notice.

He was linked with several Premier League teams, but it wasn't until March 2002 that he was tempted away from Preston by Everton.

David Moyes and Everton Football Club was a perfect match from the moment that the Scot breezed through the doors of Goodison Park for his very first press conference and he declared the Blues to be 'The People's Club.'

"This is the People's Club in Liverpool," he said. "The people on the street support Everton and I hope to give them something they can be proud of over the next few years."

He certainly did that... and it didn't take him long to get started!

Everton welcomed Fulham to Goodison Park for Moyes's first game and they took the lead through David Unsworth after just 32 seconds!

The new era was under way and Everton secured a most important victory.

In his first full season, 2002/2003, he gave a 16-year-old called Wayne Rooney his professional debut as he steered the club to a seventh-placed finish.

That was one of nine seasons in which Everton finished in the Premier League's top eight during Moyes first spell—including 2004/05 when the team qualified for the Champions League by finishing fourth in the table.

Everton also reached the FA Cup final in 2009, losing to Chelsea, and reached the semi-final in 2012.

Moyes was named as the LMA Manager of the Year on three occasions—2003, 2005 and 2009—before being lured away by Manchester United as the direct replacement for Sir Alex Ferguson.

Since then, he has been in charge of Real Sociedad, Sunderland and West Ham United—winning the 2024 European Conference League trophy with the Hammers.

But throughout his managerial travels, Everton stayed in his heart and when he was invited back to Goodison in January 2025 to replace Sean Dyche, he didn't hesitate.

Once again, he had a quick influence on results and steered the team away from the relegation zone to mid-table security.

In the summer of 2025, Moyes was awarded an OBE for his services to football—receiving the medal from Prince William.

After the Buckingham Palace ceremony, he said: "It was a great honour to be given an OBE today. It was a really special day for me and my family. It was the first time I'd met Prince William and he congratulated me on how well we'd done at Everton."

QUIZ QUESTIONS!

How well do you know David Moyes...

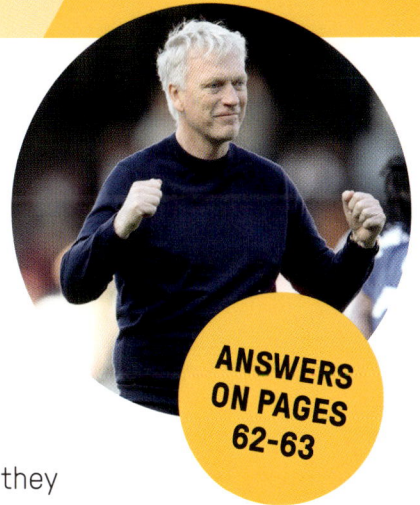

ANSWERS ON PAGES 62-63

1) Which of the Glasgow giants did Moyes play for—Celtic or Rangers?

2) What was his position on the pitch when he was a player?

3) When Moyes led Everton to the 2009 FA Cup final, who did they beat on penalties in the semi-final?

4) And which future Everton manager scored the winning goal in that 2009 final?

5) Moyes's first win of his second Everton spell last season was 3-2 at Goodison against which London team?

6) Under Moyes, Everton won their last three games of last season against which teams?

BACKROOM STAFF

ALAN IRVINE

Alan Irvine has served Everton Football Club in just about every conceivable capacity. He first came to Merseyside from Scottish outfit Queens Park in 1981, making his Blues debut in December against Aston Villa at Goodison Park.

He made 79 appearances for Everton, including the first ever Merseyside derby at Wembley when Everton met Liverpool in the League Cup final in 1984.

He scored six goals but started to find first-team opportunities hard to come by and left Goodison for Crystal Palace in 1984. After further playing spells at Dundee United and Blackburn Rovers he moved into coaching and served Blackburn Rovers and Newcastle United before becoming David Moyes' number two at Everton in 2002.

He left Everton again in 2007 to become the manager of Preston North End and had a further period in charge of Sheffield Wednesday before returning to Everton in 2011 as Academy Director.

Three years later, Irvine accepted the opportunity to manage West Bromwich Albion in the Premier League and later coached at Norwich City and West Ham United before coming to Everton for a fourth spell when David Moyes was re-appointed as manager in 2025.

BILLY MCKINLAY

Born in Glasgow, McKinlay started his professional playing career with Dundee United, where he was a teammate of a young Duncan Ferguson. After more than 280 appearances, he was tempted south of the border and joined Blackburn Rovers in 1995. Rovers were the Premier League champions at the time.

By then, McKinlay was a full Scottish international and would eventually win 29 caps for his country, playing at Euro 96 and the 1998 World Cup.

After Blackburn, he played for Bradford City, Preston North End (where he was signed by David Moyes), Clydebank, Leicester City and Fulham.

Since retiring from playing McKinlay has enjoyed a lengthy coaching career with Fulham, Watford, Stabaek (Norway), Sunderland, Stoke City and West Ham United, before coming to Everton in January 2025.

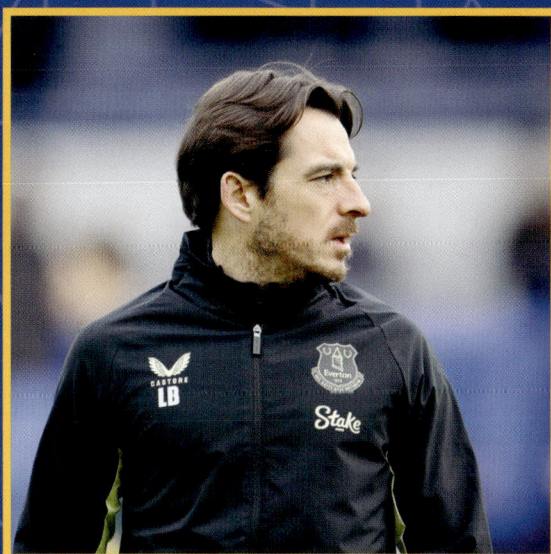

LEIGHTON BAINES

Leighton Baines joined Everton from Wigan Athletic in 2006 and went on to become one of the best left-backs the club has ever had.

He played 420 times for the Blues, a tally that leaves him 14th on the club's all-time appearance list, scoring 39 goals along the way.

In 2009 he played in every round as Everton reached the FA Cup final, scoring one of the penalties in the semi-final shoot-out victory over Manchester United at Wembley.

He was named as Everton's Player of the Season in 2011 and 2013, and the Players' Player of the Season in 2010, 2011 and 2013.

Also in 2011, he won the Everton Goal of the Season award for a stunning free-kick in the last minute of extra-time against Chelsea in an FA Cup tie.

Baines played 30 times for England, including two games in the 2014 World Cup in Brazil.

After coaching with the Blues Academy, he accepted a first-team role when David Moyes returned to the club.

HILL DICKINSON STADIUM OPENS ITS DOORS!

The magnificent Hill Dickinson Stadium staged Premier League football for the very first time in August 2025. Brighton & Hove Albion were the visitors and although it marked the end of the construction journey on the banks of the River Mersey, it was very much the start of a new and exciting era for Everton Football Club...

1 Earlier in the week, the finishing touches were put to the huge crests that adorn the external walls of the stadium.

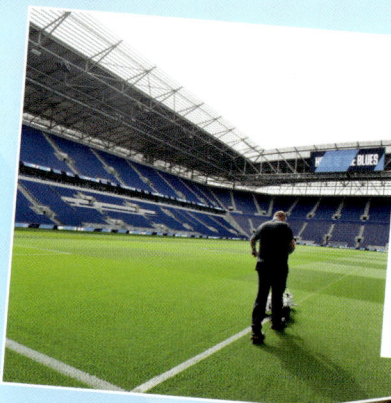

2 Amongst the first in on the special matchday are the hardworking ground staff to make sure that the pitch is in perfect playing condition.

3 The concourses at Hill Dickinson Stadium are much wider than those at Goodison Park...

4 ...and the turnstile entrances are a bit different too!

5 A few hours before the kick-off and the first fans start to arrive. Plenty get there early to soak up the atmosphere on this historic day.

6 The replica of the famous Littlewoods Clock that was at Goodison Park for decades is a lovely centrepiece in the brand-new Club Store at Hill Dickinson Stadium.

7 Some fans took the opportunity to look for their commemorative stone on Everton Way. Duncan Ferguson won't have to look too hard!

8 This is where the players will enter the stadium and make their way to the home dressing room...

9 ...which is spic and span waiting for the arrival of the players.

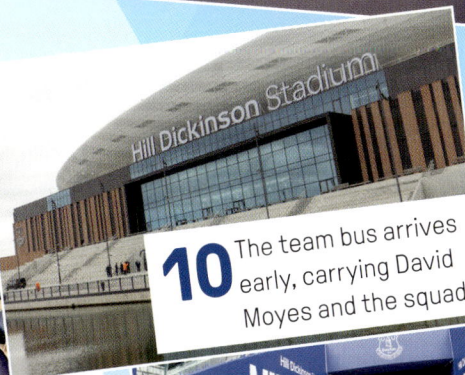

10 The team bus arrives early, carrying David Moyes and the squad...

11 ...but there are still some enthusiastic fans waiting to greet them as they leave the bus and head into the stadium.

12 This is where the players will walk out before the start of the game.

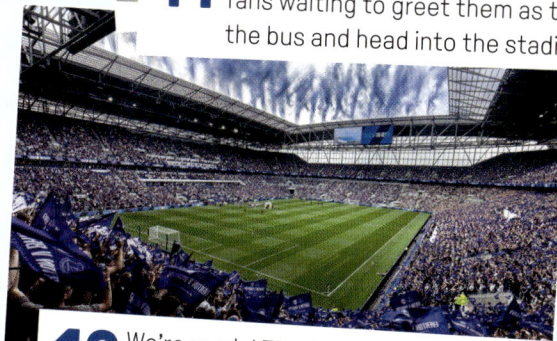

13 We're ready! The flags are waving and the sky is blue with the smoke of the fireworks. History is about to be made!

14 Iliman Ndiaye scored the very last Premier League goal at Goodison Park... and he also gets the very first one at Hill Dickinson Stadium.

15 James Garner scored the second goal in the 2-0 win, and he speaks to the television cameras after the final whistle.

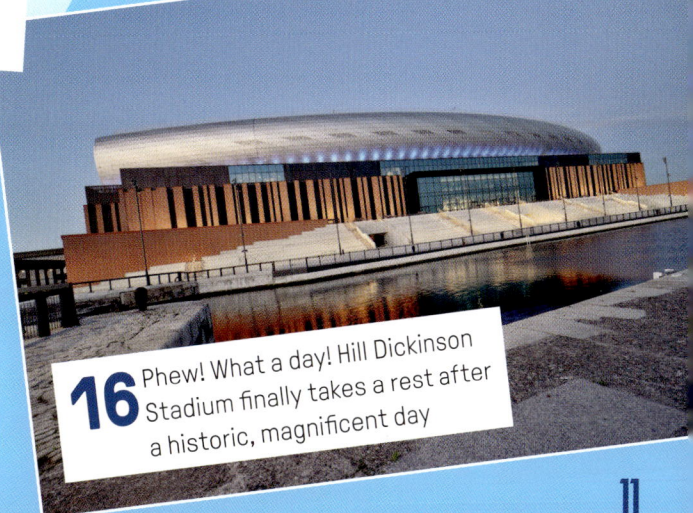

16 Phew! What a day! Hill Dickinson Stadium finally takes a rest after a historic, magnificent day

QUIZ

See how much you remember about the 2024/25 season...

ANSWERS ON PAGES 62-63

1 In the summer before the start of the season, England lost 2-1 in the European Championship final to Spain. Who scored the Three Lions' goal?

2 Name the two teams who were beaten in the 2025 FA Cup semi-finals?

3 Leighton Baines and Seamus Coleman were in charge for an FA Cup 3rd round tie at Goodison Park against which team?

4 Which team knocked Everton out of the FA Cup?

5 Who won the Carabao Cup final in March 2025?

6 The top-scoring English international in the Premier League with 16 goals was which Aston Villa striker?

7 Who was Everton's top goalscorer in all competitions last season?

8 Which two teams did Everton beat by a 4-0 scoreline at Goodison Park?

9 Which three teams were relegated from the Premier League?

10 Jordan Pickford kept 12 Premier League clean sheets last term—only two keepers kept more. One plays for Arsenal and one for Nottingham Forest. Can you name them both?

11 Which three teams were promoted from the Championship to the Premier League?

12 Which two teams contested the UEFA Champions League final?

13 And what was the final score in that game?

14 Which two English teams contested the Europa League final?

15 Chelsea won the Europa Conference League by beating which team 4-1?

Q3

Q9

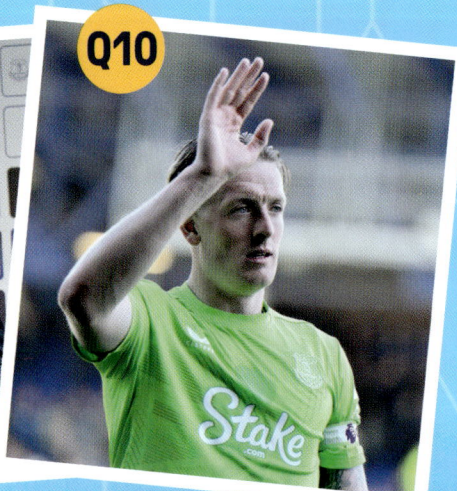

Q10

STAR PLAYER!

JARRAD BRANTHWAITE

Just about the best news of the summer of 2025 was Jarrad Branthwaite putting an end to all the transfer speculation by signing at new contract with Everton!

The big defender has been a revelation for the Blues after forcing his way into the team and Everton supporters all across the world rejoiced when it was confirmed that he was going nowhere!

Branthwaite was born in Carlisle in June 2002 and started his career with his hometown team, Carlisle United.

In January 2020 he made the big move to Everton, making his debut under the legendary manager Carlo Ancelotti against Wolverhampton Wanderers in an empty stadium during the days when the Covid pandemic meant that nobody could go to the games.

Branthwaite played a few more games but then really felt the benefit of a couple of loan moves – first to Blackburn Rovers and then to Dutch giants PSV Eindhoven.

When he came back to Everton, he was ready!

So much so, that he forced his way into the England squad, making his full international debut in June 2024 against Bosnia & Herzegovina.

He's also proved himself to be a man for the big occasion, scoring vital goals against Chelsea, Tottenham Hotspur and, of course, Liverpool!

He was delighted, therefore, to put pen to paper on his new deal.

"The past two years have been massive for me on a personal note," he said. "The trust the Club's put in me and how many games I've played over the past two seasons, it made it quite an easy decision for me to stay and to keep progressing as a player. It's the perfect platform for me to do that.

"For me, as a player, it's about playing as many games as I can. I know the Club, I feel loved by the fans and the players, and the group we've got is a good group. Also, obviously, with the new

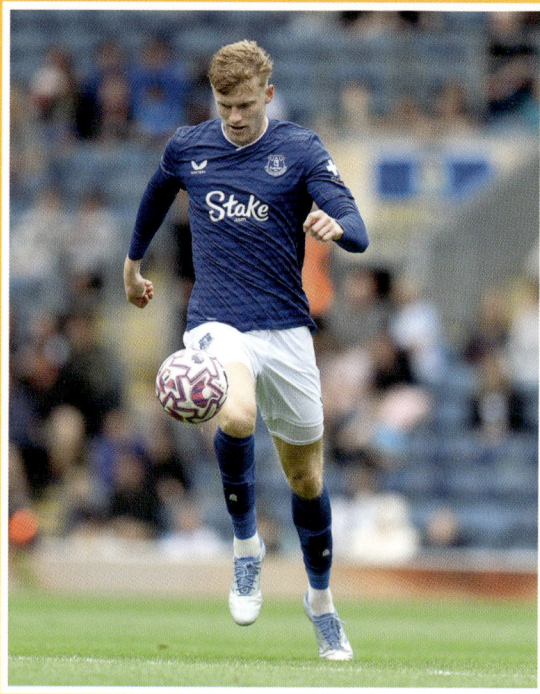

ownership and the new manager coming in, it's an exciting project and it's something that I want to be part of."

Solid performances and vital goals have certainly made Branthwaite a big fans favourite and he appreciates the following that the magnificent supporters give to him and the rest of the players.

"It's massive and over the past few years I've seen the impact that the fans have on us as a team and how much it means to them," he said.

"I've seen the change the Club's had and it's very exciting for us, as players, to have that going on in the background and obviously to start the new season at the new stadium was a big thing for us."

Branthwaite is also grateful for the help and advice he gets from the players around him, both on the pitch and on the training ground.

"Yeah, definitely. Jordan Pickford has played for England so many times, he is so experienced, and Tarky has played so many games in the Premier League. When you're a young player, it's good to have those types of players around you. They've helped me over the past two seasons and I think generally as a group we work well together so hopefully that can continue.

"I feel I've got the experience that I need now. I'd played over 75 games before the start of this season (86 actually Jarrad!!) and I think something I can improve on is to maybe be more of a leader in the team. If I bring that into my game, that will not only help me but the team."

After breaking through into the England squad, Branthwaite was disappointed not to be included in the Euro 24 squad (and Evertonians were shocked!) but he has his sights on the 2026 World Cup.

"That's something I'll be pushing for throughout the season, to give myself the best possible chance to be in that squad," he said.

"The only person that can get you in that (England) team is yourself. It's about how you perform and how the results are on the pitch. I've learnt so much from when I first started and you know you're always going to improve. You're also going to make mistakes and it's about how you react and learn from them, which I have done. Now I'm just focusing on keeping improving as a player and seeing where that takes me."

One man who can certainly help Branthwaite to just keep improving is, of course, the manager, David Moyes. He came back to Everton in January 2025 and his impact was immediate.

"Since he came in he's been really good, not only for me but for the group," said Branthwaite. "You saw the change in results and the change in mood. He drives us and demands every day to be better."

If David Moyes can make Jarrad Branthwaite better and better every day, then we've all got a lot to look forward to!

VITALII
MYKOLENKO

NAME THE PLAYER

These ten players all played against Everton in the Premier League during the 2024/25 season. How many of them (and their teams) can you name?

1

2

3

4

5

6

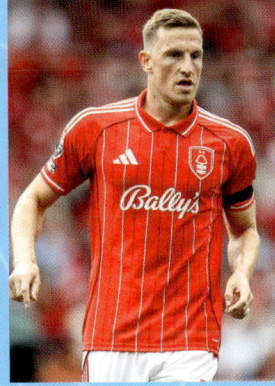

7

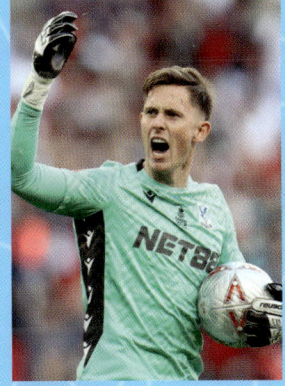

8

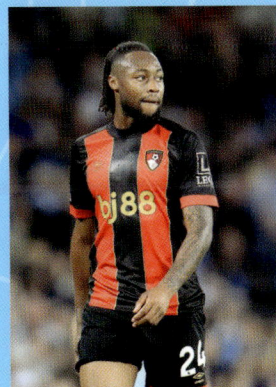

9

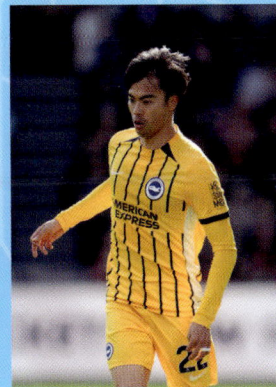

10

ANSWERS ON PAGES 62-63

THINGS YOU DIDN'T KNOW THAT YOU DIDN'T KNOW ABOUT GOODISON PARK!

Everton played 2,791 games at Goodison across all competitions. Technically, two of them were as the away team. In the 1991 FA Cup 4th round we were drawn away to Woking, but the tie was switched to Goodison by the non-league side for financial reasons. Likewise, Bury played their 1912 FA Cup 2nd round replay at L4 rather than at Gigg Lane.

Everton won 1538 games at Goodison, scoring 5370 goals and conceding 3028.

Our longest ever home winning streak was between October 1930 and April 1931 when we were victorious in 17 Goodison games!

In total, 856 players represented Everton at Goodison Park, with Neville Southall playing there more than anyone else. Big Nev made 376 home appearances.

Needless to say, the game's greatest ever goalscorer, William Ralph Dixie Dean, is Goodison's leading marksman and it's highly unlikely that his tally of 241 will ever be beaten.

The highest scoring games at Goodison were a 9-3 win against Sheffield Wednesday in 1931 and an 8-4 success over Plymouth Argyle in 1954.

The most regular visitors to Goodison Park were Liverpool, who played us on our patch no less than 120 times. James Tarkowski scored the last ever Merseyside derby goal!

Liverpool were our opponents when Goodison recorded its highest ever attendance. 78,299 spectators saw the September 1948 derby – which is double the capacity for the stadium's final season.

Our most popular opponents were Sunderland, who we defeated 60 times at Goodison. The 216 goals we put past the Black Cats in those matches is also a record.

Nottingham Forest were our first competitive opponents back in 1892 and, of course, the last visitors were Southampton. Altogether, 148 different teams played Everton at Goodison.

The fastest ever first-team Goodison goal was scored after 10 seconds by Abdoulaye Doucoure against Leicester City in February 2025. There was a quicker strike during an FA Youth Cup game in December 1969 by Everton's David Johnson, officially timed by the club at five seconds!

The latest goal was Alex Iwobi's 99th-minute winner against Newcastle United in March 2022.

Goodison played host to 18 international matches, including five in the 1966 World Cup.

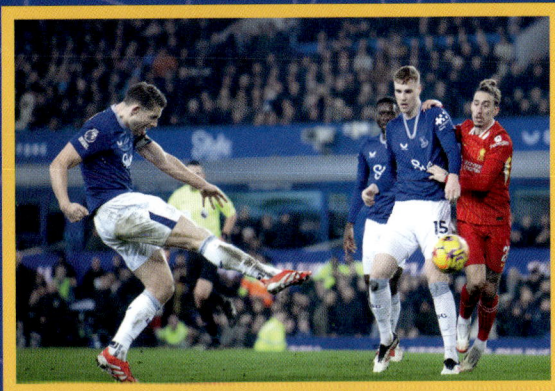

When Everton played Barnsley at Goodison in the FA Cup in 1915, the Blues ended up with just SEVEN players left on the pitch. We had two men sent off and, in the days before substitutes, two left the pitch through injury. Everton still won 3-0!

Goodison is the only ground where more than one goalkeeper has netted in the Premier League. Peter Schmeichel scored for Aston Villa in 2001 and Tim Howard against Bolton Wanderers in 2012.

In 1981, there was a £250 prize for the winner of the Golden Goal competition—punters purchased a ticket with a goal time and if it matched the actual first goal, you won the prize. Against Notts County in September 1981, the winner was… Alex Ferguson! He was on a scouting mission as manager of Aberdeen!

IDRISSA
GANA GUEYE

ISAAC HEATH

When did you start playing football?

Probably when I was about 4-years-old, in our back garden in Leeds, kicking a ball about with my dad. He never played football, but he gave me a ball and I took to it. Later on, my mum didn't know what to do with me during the summer, so she took me to a soccer camp and I did well and pushed on from there.

When did you come to Everton?

I was playing for Leeds United Academy against Everton and one of the Everton guys approached me. I'd been at Leeds from 9 until I was 13. I played with Archie Gray when I was at Leeds – he's at Tottenham Hotspur now. Jensen Metcalfe and Roman Dixon were in the Everton team when I got here.

I enjoyed it at Leeds but when I came to Everton, everything was on point – the sports science, the nutrition, the GPS vests, it was all there for the young players and I felt myself starting to improve as soon as I got started.

You joined Everton at 13, so did your family have to move from Leeds to Liverpool?

No! My dad would take time off work and drive me from Leeds for training three or four times a week. That's a lot of travelling! I'd make the journey straight after school and I'd fall asleep on the way home every day! That stopped when I signed my scholarship at 16 and the Club put me in with a host family. It was tough because I couldn't drive at the time so there wasn't a lot for me to do, apart from

the training. There were two of us young players in the house with the family.

When did you first play for the Under-21s?
When I was a second year scholar at the age of 17. I had known Paul Tait (Under-21s manager) from younger age groups and he's been great with me all the way through. It was a big step up to play for the 21s. The training and the games had more intensity and there was more pressure to perform.

And what about when you get the chance to train with the first team?
It's great! I like the intensity of the training sessions because everyone is always demanding more and that suits me. I like to be put under pressure. I never used to be like that, but I realised that I need to be challenged to improve. The first team players were very good with me, but they'll also tell you when you're not doing well because they have such high standards.

You travelled with the first team to the USA in the summer of 2025. That must have been a great experience?
Yes it was, but some of the training was tough because of the very hot weather. It gave a few of us younger players the chance to see how senior players conduct themselves during a long pre-season trip. That's all part of the learning curve. It was great to get some game time in the States as well...I'd never played in front of so many people! But once I got my first touch on the ball, I was fine. I started to thrive off the energy that was coming from the crowd.

What are your attributes as a player?
I like to dribble and I like to pass the ball. I also think I've got a good work ethic; I always try to give everything I've got for the team. I'd like to score more goals though! But I've always got as much joy from an assist as I have from scoring myself.

It's not easy to become a professional footballer is it?
You have to grow up quickly when you are in football and you have to keep improving as a person as well as a player. You have to make a lot of sacrifices along the way. I didn't have a normal childhood like most kids because I was so dedicated and driven to be a footballer. I knew I had one shot at it so I would always be the kid training in the park instead of going out with my mates. It was tough at times but I had my vision. It's been a good journey for me and I want to continue to push on.

HISTORY LESSON

You'll probably need a grown-up to help you with this quiz –unless, of course, you'd rather be the Quizmaster! These are all former players who were invited to Goodison Park in May 2025 for the stadium's last ever Premier League fixture. They were all paraded around the pitch after the final whistle and the crowd loved it! Look at the photographs, read the clues and see who can recognise the former players.

ANSWERS ON PAGES 62-63

01

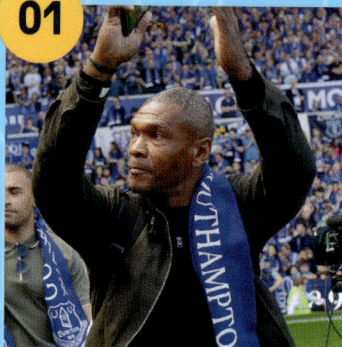

I signed for Everton from Ipswich Town in 2004.

....

03

I played in the 1995 FA Cup final—and the 1994 World Cup for Sweden!

....

05

Only Romelu Lukaku has scored more Premier League goals for Everton than me.

....

02

I'm on the left and won the Premier League before joining Everton in 2013—my mate on the right won it after he left!

....

04

Born and bred an Evertonian, I was 17 when I made my first-team debut.

....

06

A Frenchman, I arrived at Goodison in 2009.

....

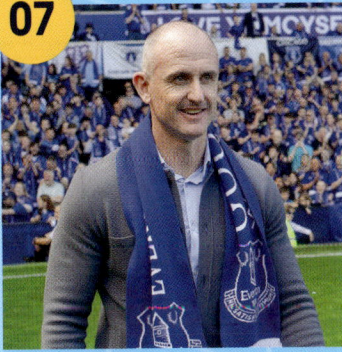

07

I scored in my one and only England international in 2004.

....

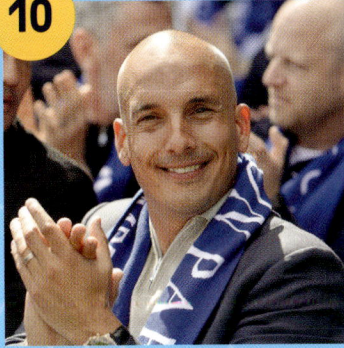

10

You will have seen me on Match of the Day!

....

13

Me and my midfield pals were known as the 'Dogs of War'.

....

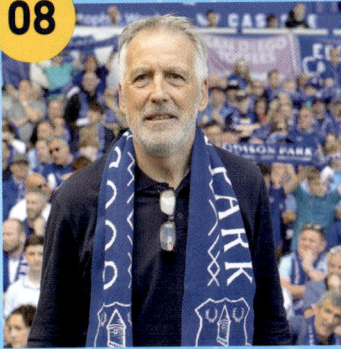

08

The fans used to sing that I could walk on water!

....

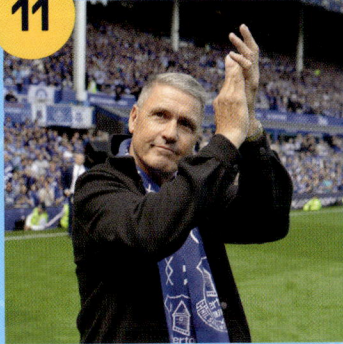

11

I scored the winning goal for Everton in an FA Cup final.

....

14

I scored a hat-trick on my Everton debut and my mate alongside me scored twice in an FA Cup final.

....

09

I once scored a perfect hat-trick against Chelsea—right foot, left foot and header.

....

12

Born in Poland, I played my international football for Canada.

....

15

I managed in the Premier League after I finished playing.

....

GETTING TO KNOW
THIERNO BARRY

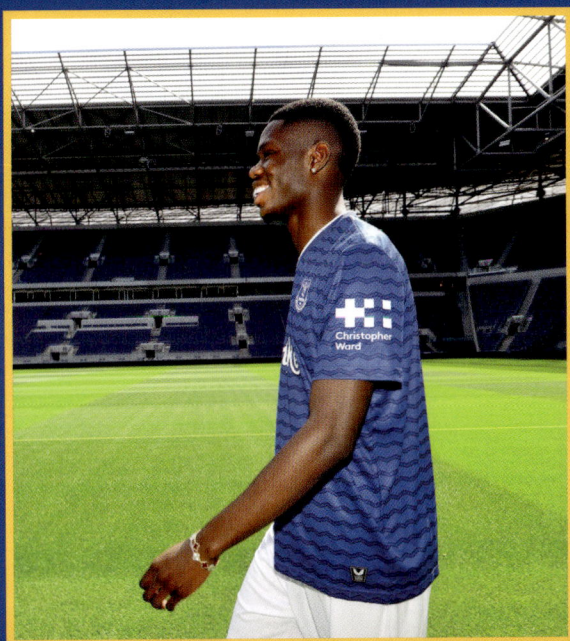

Remember when Wayne Rooney scored THAT goal against Arsenal—his first one in the Premier League at the age of 16 on 19 October 2002. Thierno Barry was born two days later in Lyon, France.

He started his playing career in the youth team at Saint-Priest, a team which is currently in the French fourth division.

Thierno's first professional club was Souchaux-Montbeliard. He played for their reserve team that competed in the French third division, but despite having a good goalscoring record he never broke into the first team.

His form didn't go unnoticed elsewhere though and in 2022 he signed for Belgian side, Beveren.

Beveren were in the second tier in Belgium and, again, Thierno scored freely, but the team just missed out on promotion.

After that one season, Thierno was on the move again—this time to Switzerland to join FC Basel. He was sent off on his debut!

The 2023/24 campaign was a challenging one for Basel. They had three different managers and finished 8th in the league. Thierno was their top scorer.

In the summer of 2024, Thierno was off to Spain! He joined La Liga outfit Villarreal.

Villarreal finished 5th in La Liga, to qualify for the Champions League, with Thierno scoring 11 goals. Only former Newcastle United and Leicester City striker Ayoze Perez scored more.

Thierno was in the Top 10 list of under-23 goalscorers in Europe's big five leagues last season—England, Italy, Spain, France and Germany. (Chelsea's Cole Palmer was joint top)

Thierno is 6'5" tall and that height makes him a huge threat in the air. He ranked second of all forwards in Europe's major leagues (and top of anyone in La Liga) for aerial duel success in 2024-25, winning 66.7% of his 153 challenges (minimum 100 aerial duels).

In 2025, Thierno was part of the France Under-21 squad that competed in the European Championships that was eventually won by Lee Carsley's England. Thierno was an unused substitute when France lost to Germany in the semi-final.

In July 2025, Thierno signed for Everton!

"I'm very happy, it's very exciting to be here," he said. "Everton is a big club in the Premier League. They have a good history and good players have played here, like Wayne Rooney and Romelu Lukaku. When I was young, I liked to watch these players, now I want to do like these players who have gone before."

SEAMUS COLEMAN'S TEAM-MATES QUIZ

"I have been fortunate enough to play alongside many players during my Everton career. Here are just ten of them – how many can you name?"

1.

2.

3.

4.

5.

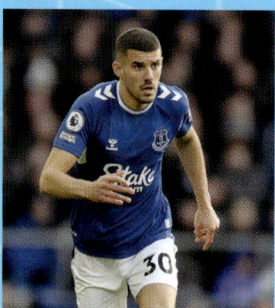

6.

7.

8.

ANSWERS ON PAGES 62-63

9.

10.

JORDAN
PICKFORD

MEET:

JACK GREALISH

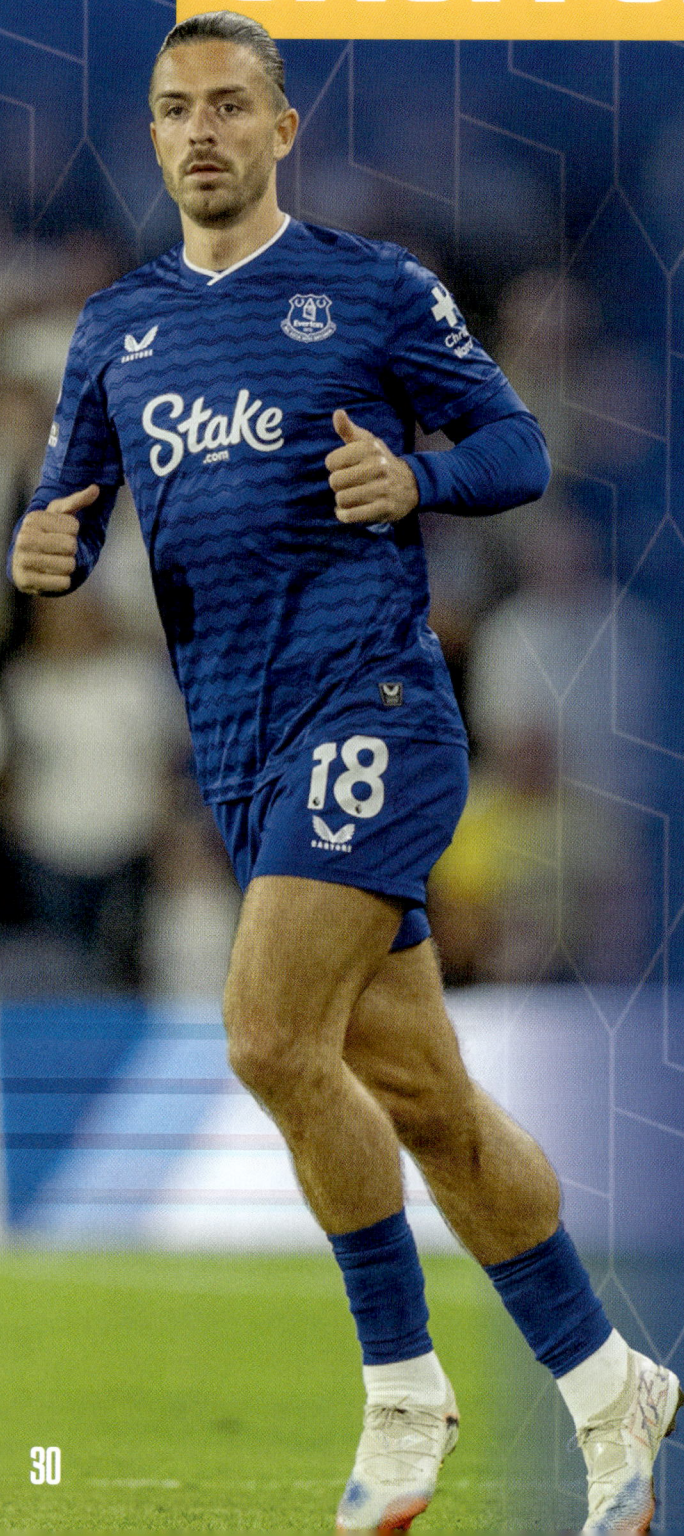

There was much excitement in the summer of 2025 when Everton signed England international Jack Grealish from Manchester City on a season-long loan. And the enthusiasm amongst the Evertonians was hardly surprising… it's not every day your club signs a £100m player!

Yet that was the fee that Pep Guardiola paid Aston Villa for Grealish in August 2021. Grealish was the hottest property in English football and he had no hesitation in taking the number 10 shirt that had previously been worn by City's record goalscorer, Sergio Aguero.

On signing for Everton four years later, Grealish took the number 18 jersey, and explained why: "There were other numbers, but my two favourite English players ever are Wayne Rooney and Paul Gascoigne and I know they both wore number 18 here. They were so fearless, they were both so good technically and both wanted to be direct and make stuff happen. So, as soon as I knew this deal was close, I had a look and number 18 was free, so that was perfect for me and it was the only number I was going to take from that point. I spoke to Wayne [Rooney] before I came here and I mentioned that to him – about the number 18 – so I hope he's happy as well!"

One man who was certainly happy was the Everton manager David Moyes.

"We welcome Jack to Everton, and we're very pleased to have him on board," he said. "I think we're getting him at a good time because he's experienced, he understands the Premier League,

and we're all fully aware of the levels he's capable of performing to.

"I know Jack's ambition is to get back into the England squad so hopefully we can help him achieve that over the course of the season. We're all looking forward to working with him and providing a platform for him to show the best version of himself."

And Grealish was equally delighted to be teaming up with the boss.

"I said to Seamus and to Tarky that when I had my first chat with the manager, that was one of the reasons why I wanted to come here. I told my agent that I didn't want to go anywhere else, I wanted to go and play for Everton. And the fans here are incredible! It was always so tough to play against Everton at Goodison Park. I'm happy now that I am ready to be on their side!"

Another person who was really pleased to see Grealish travel down the M62 from Manchester to Merseyside was England's number one, Jordan Pickford. They know each other well from international call-ups and Grealish revealed that the keeper was determined to help him join the Blues!

"I had a lot of chats with Pickers!" he grinned. "He was face-timing me from the golf course asking me if I'd signed yet! He's an incredible goalkeeper, one of the best I've ever played with for sure. He only said good words about this

football club and I am delighted to be on his side."

Jack Grealish was born in Birmingham on 10 September 1995, four months after Everton had beaten Manchester United in the FA Cup final at Wembley! At the age of just six, he was already showing potential as a footballer and he joined Aston Villa's Academy.

In March 2012, when he was still only 16, he was an unused substitute when Villa played Chelsea in the Premier League. Eighteen months later he was loaned out to Notts County to get some first-team experience and made his senior professional debut as a substitute in a 3-1 away win at MK Dons.

In May 2014 Grealish made his Aston Villa debut against, ironically, Manchester City. Whilst at Villa Park, he played in an FA Cup final, a League Cup final and a Championship play-off final.

But it was at Manchester City when his trophy cabinet started to fill up. Grealish won the Premier League title in three successive seasons, 2022, 2023 and 2024, the FA Cup and UEFA Champions League in 2023, and the UEFA Super Cup and FIFA World Club Cup in the same year!

On the international stage, Grealish played youth football for the Republic of Ireland, even up to the Under-21s, but in 2015 he declared that his future allegiance would be with England. He played Under-21 football for the Three Lions and made his senior debut in August 2020 against Denmark, alongside Jordan Pickford. Future Everton defender Conor Coady made his England debut in the same game.

When he joined The Toffees, Grealish had won 39 caps, scoring four goals.

GREALISH'S CAREER IN PICTURES

1. Before making his debut for Aston Villa, Jack was loaned out to Notts County for some first team experience.

2. Following a successful loan spell at Meadow Lane, Jack returned to Aston Villa and forced his way into the first team. Here he is in action against Steven Naismith.

3. In 2015, Jack played for Aston Villa in the FA Cup final at Wembley, but his team was soundly beaten by Arsenal.

4. In September 2015, he scored his first goal for Villa – away at Leicester City.

5. In 2019 Jack was named in the Championship Team of the Year at the annual Professional Footballers' Association (PFA) awards evening.

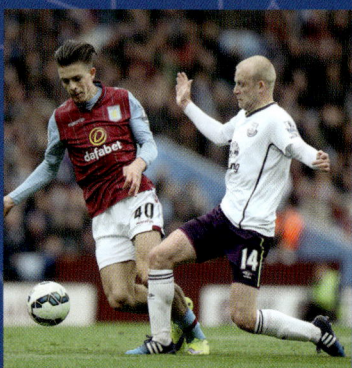

6. Jack made his England debut in September 2020, away at Denmark. The game ended 0-0 and he came off the bench in the second half to replace Kalvin Philips.

7. In October 2021, Jack scored his first international goal. England defeated Andorra 5-0 in a World Cup qualifier, with Jack scoring the fifth, four minutes from time.

8. In the summer of 2021, Jack was part of the England squad that reached the final of the Covid-delayed European Championships.

9. In 2021, Jack signed for Manchester City.

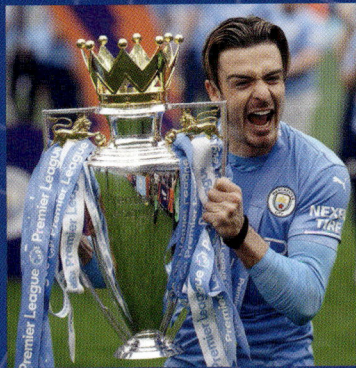

10. At the end of his first season at the Etihad, Jack was a Premier League champion!

11. In 2023, Jack was finally an FA Cup winner as Manchester City beat rivals Manchester United in the final at Wembley.

12. 2023 was a treble year for Jack as City also won the UEFA Champions League, defeating Inter Milan in the final in Turkey.

13. In August 2025, Jack signed a one-year loan deal with Everton!

14. The next day he visited Hill Dickinson Stadium for the very first time – and enjoyed the reflective glass in the Tunnel Club area!

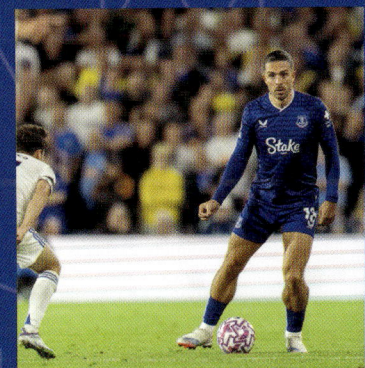

15. He made his Blues debut against Leeds United at Elland Road. Everton lost but...

16. ...when Jack played at Hill Dickinson Stadium for the first time, he set up both goals in a 2-0 victory against Brighton & Hove Albion!

FANS PHOTO GALLERY

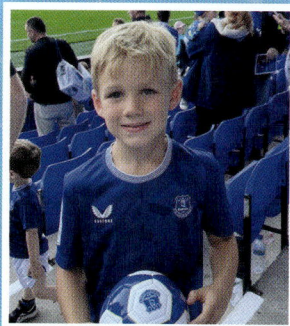

Quinn

Bella

Charlie

Roman

Evie

Albie

Tara & Kian

Jasmine

Max & Violet

Max

Olly

Darcy

Isla

Thomas

Aiden & Louie

Erin

Freddie

Jack & Alfie

Joshus, Isaac & Noah

Leo & Finley

Jacob

Fray, Lockie & Dixon

Aoife & Finian

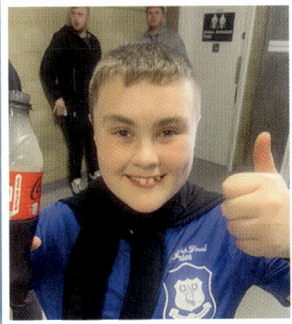
Ryan

Owen

Liana

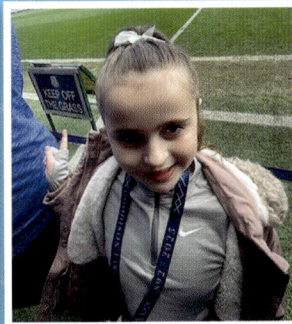
Chloe

Archie

Thomas

George

Lillie-Rae

Buddy

Thomas & Noah

Evie

Willow

Oscar

Charlie

FANS PHOTO GALLERY

Oliver

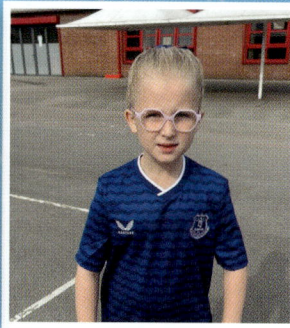
Melodie

Joseph

Ava

Lewis & Bonnie

Ethan

Theo

Eliza & Reggie

Sylvie

Isla & Edith

Millie

Shane

Jacob

Alana & Poppy

Ella

Davie

Thomas

Kara

Jack

Hayden

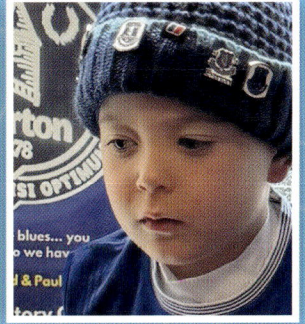
Arnie

Stan

Isaac

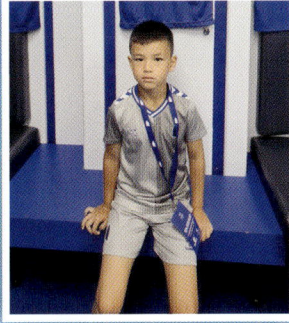
Jayden

Freddie

Poppy

Leighton

Oliver

Reuben

Jude & India

Isabella

Arthur

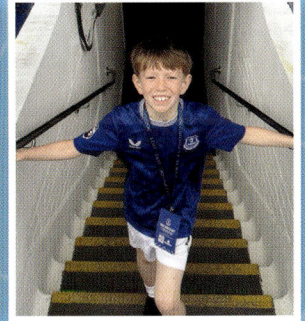
Otis

Luca

Henry

Alfie & Charlie

Louie

GUESS THE JOURNEY!

ANSWERS ON PAGES 62-63

Name the current Everton players from their previous clubs... with a nice easy one to start!

1 Sligo Rovers, EVERTON

2 Sheffield United, Hyde United (loan), Marseilles, EVERTON

3 Burnley, EVERTON

4 Oldham Athletic, Brentford, Burnley, EVERTON

5 Racing Club, Southampton, Juventus (loan), Flamengo, EVERTON

6 Manchester United, Watford (loan), Nottingham Forest (loan), EVERTON

7 Lille, Aston Villa, Everton, Paris St Germain, EVERTON

8 Dynamo Kyiv, EVERTON

9 Sunderland, Darlington (loan), Alfreton Town (loan) Burton Albion (loan), Carlisle United (loan), Bradford City (loan), Preston North End (loan), EVERTON

10 Manchester United, Leicester City (loan), Derby County (loan), Blackburn Rovers (loan), Burnley, EVERTON

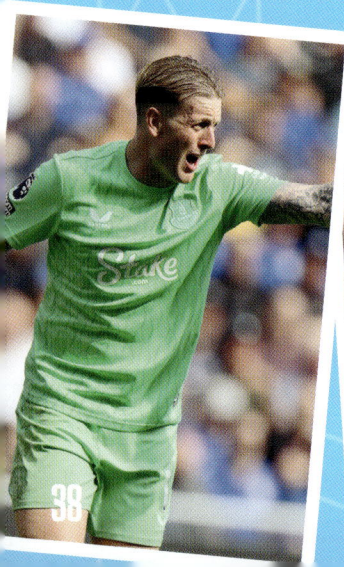

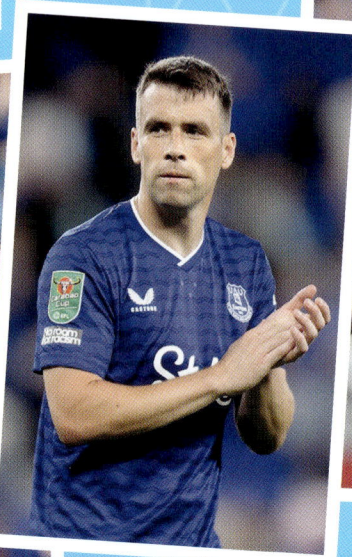

TIM
IROEGBUNAM

HAPPY BIRTHDAY!!!

HARRISON ARMSTRONG – 19TH JANUARY

BETO – 31ST JANUARY

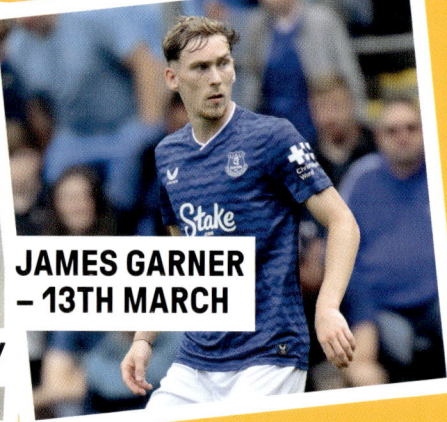

JAMES GARNER – 13TH MARCH

DAVID MOYES – 25TH APRIL

JAKE O'BRIEN – 15TH MAY

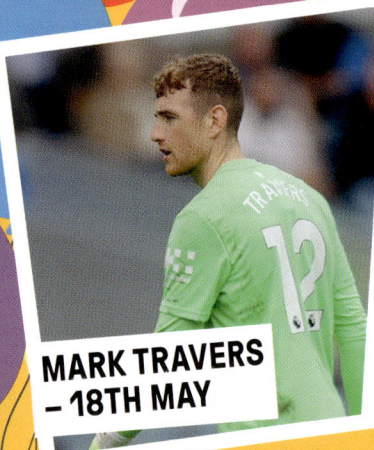

MARK TRAVERS – 18TH MAY

VITALII MYKOLENKO – 29TH MAY

JAMES TARKOWSKI – 19TH NOVEMBER

Do you share a birthday with one of your favourite players...?

MICHAEL KEANE – 11TH JANUARY
TYLER DIBLING – 17TH FEBRUARY
ILIMAN NDIAYE – 6TH MARCH
JORDAN PICKFORD – 7TH MARCH
TOM KING – 9TH MARCH
ADAM AZNOU – 2ND JUNE
JARRAD BRANTHWAITE – 27TH JUNE
TIM IROEGBUNAM – 30TH JUNE
MERLIN RÖHL - 5TH JULY
KIERNAN DEWSBURY-HALL – 6TH SEPTEMBER
JACK GREALISH – 10TH SEPTEMBER
IDRISSA GANA GUEYE – 26TH SEPTEMBER
SEAMUS COLEMAN – 11TH OCTOBER
NATHAN PATTERSON – 16TH OCTOBER
THIERNO BARRY – 21ST OCTOBER
DWIGHT MCNEIL – 22ND NOVEMBER
CHARLY ALCARAZ – 30TH NOVEMBER

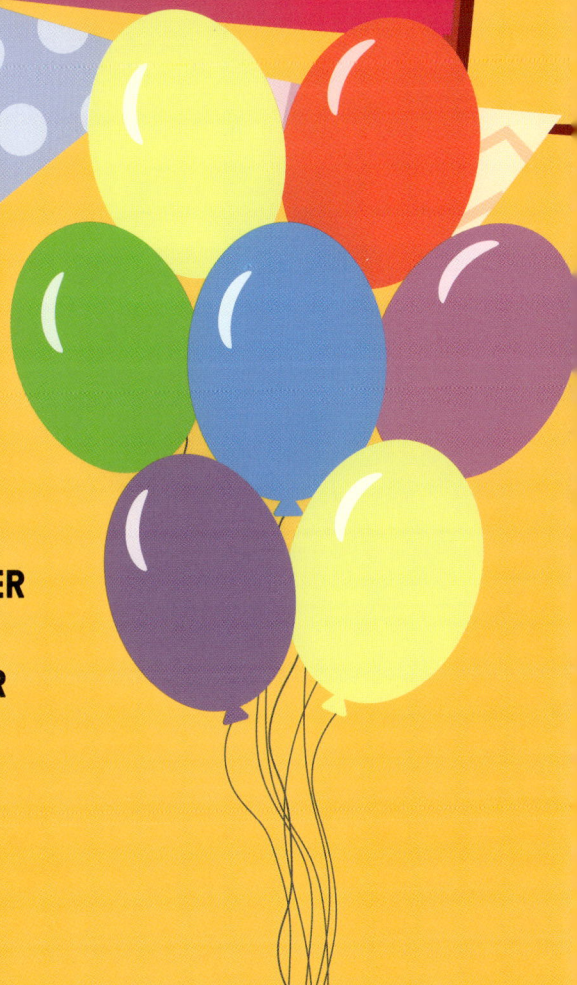

Don't forget anyone's Birthday! Make a list here of family and friends' birthdays (and your own of course) so that you remember to get them an Everton birthday card!

NAME	BIRTHDAY

GETTING TO KNOW

KIERNAN DEWSBURY-HALL

Kiernan was born in Nottingham on 6 September 1998.

At the age of six he joined a local team called Shepshed Dynamo Warriors and two years later he switched to the Leicester City Academy.

He made his first team debut for The Foxes against Brentford in an FA Cup tie in January 2020, coming off the bench to replace Kelechi Iheanacho.

After that first game he did what Seamus Coleman once did – he signed on-loan for Blackpool!

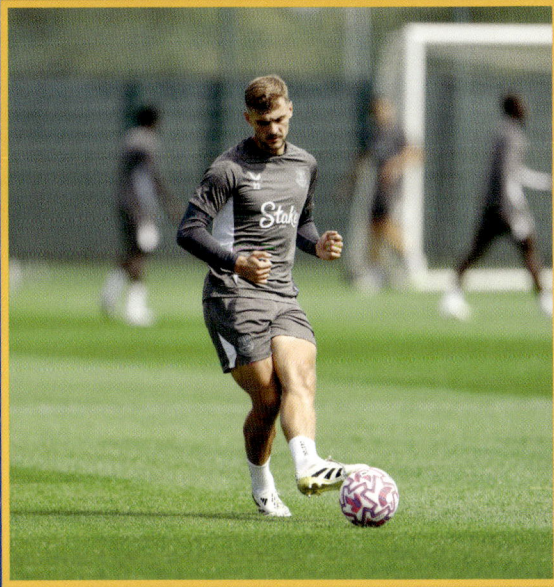

The Covid pandemic brought an end to his stay at Blackpool and he later had another loan spell with Luton Town.

At the end of his season with Luton he was voted as their Players' Player of the Season.

Back at Leicester City, Kiernan played in the 2021 Community Shield at Wembley. He came on as a substitute to replace Ayoze Perez in their 1-0 victory against Manchester City.

In December 2021, Kiernan scored his first goal for Leicester in a Europa League tie against Italian side, Napoli.

After Leicester were relegated in 2023, Kiernan stayed with them and helped them to promotion back to the Premier League. He was named as their Player of the Season and was included in the EFL Championship Team of the Season.

In July 2024, he left Leicester and joined Chelsea to rejoin his former Foxes manager Enzo Maresca.

Despite not playing regularly in the Premier League for the Londoners, Kiernan was the only player to feature in every one of their Europa Conference matches – setting up one of the goals in their 4-1 final victory against Sevilla.

In August 2025, he joined Everton and made his debut in the opening game of the season against Leeds United.

On arrival at Everton, Kiernan was given the number 22 jersey. Can you name these players who have also worn that squad number for the Blues?

01

02

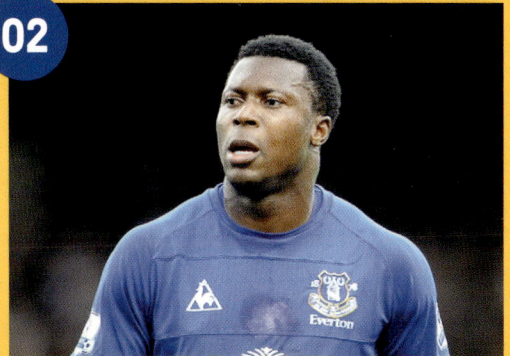

03

04

ANSWERS ON PAGES 62-63

NAME THE GROUND

Here are fifteen Premier League grounds that Everton will be playing at this season. See how many of them you can name...

01

02

03

04

05

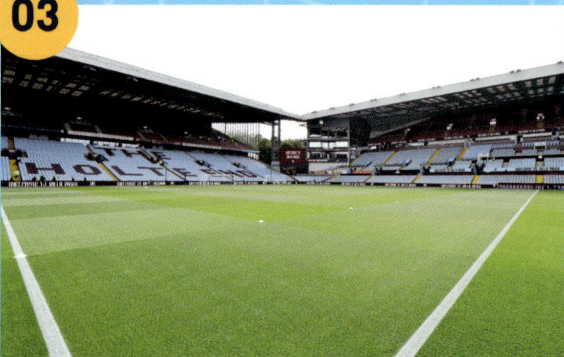

06

07

08

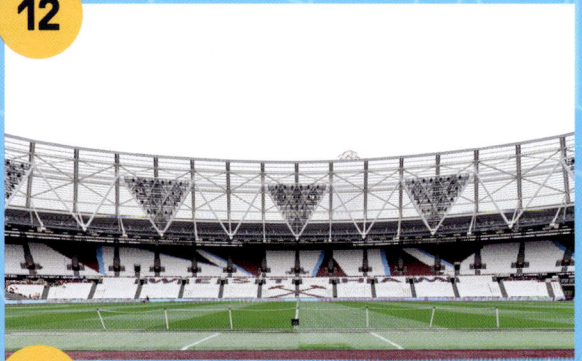

09

10

11

12

13

14

15

ANSWERS ON PAGES 62-63

ORNELLA
VIGNOLA

EVERTON WOMEN FIXTURES

Here's where and when you can watch our fabulous Everton Women's team this season – but don't forget to check evertonfc.com for any potential changes to the schedule!

SEPTEMBER
7: LIVERPOOL (Anfield)
14: TOTTENHAM HOTSPUR (Goodison Park)
21: LONDON CITY LIONESSES (Goodison Park)
28: BRIGHTON & HOVE ALBION (Broadfield Stadium)

OCTOBER
5: LEICESTER CITY (King Power Stadium)
12: MANCHESTER UNITED (Hill Dickinson Stadium)

NOVEMBER
2: ASTON VILLA (Villa Park)
9: MANCHESTER CITY (Goodison Park)
16: WEST HAM UNITED (Chigwell Construction Stadium)

DECEMBER
6: CHELSEA (Kingsmeadow)
14: ARSENAL (Goodison Park)

JANUARY
11: MANCHESTER CITY (Joie Stadium)
25: BRIGHTON & HOVE ALBION (Goodison Park)

FEBRUARY
1: ASTON VILLA (Goodison Park)
8: LONDON LIONESSES (Copperjax Community Stadium)
15: WEST HAM UNITED (Goodison Park)

MARCH
15: TOTTENHAM HOTSPUR (BetWright Stadium)
21: MANCHESTER UNITED (Leigh Sports Village)
29: LIVERPOOL (Goodison Park)

APRIL
26: CHELSEA (Goodison Park)

MAY
3: ARSENAL (Emirates Stadium)
16: LEICESTER CITY (Goodison Park)

EVERTON WOMEN

Everton Women prepared for the 2025/26 season with a plethora of new signings—including three highly-rated Japanese internationals.

Defender Hikaru Kitagawa arrived from Swedish club BK Häcken, Rion Ishikawa from Urawa Red Diamonds and Yuka Momiki from Leicester City.

Regarded as one of world football's best full-backs, Kitagawa was crucial to Japan's 2025 SheBelieves Cup victory. The defender lifted the trophy alongside new Blues teammates Ishikawa and Honoka Hayashi, who joined from West Ham United in 2024.

Kitagawa started her career at the JFA Academy Fukushima and played for Japan at youth level, before homeland spells with Urawa Reds, Albirex Niigata and INAC Kobe Leonessa. Her first taste of European football came in 2024 with BK Häcken in Sweden after she had impressed for Japan at the Olympic Games in France.

Central defender, Ishikawa, also started her football journey at the JFA Academy before joining Urawa Red Diamonds in 2022. That same year she represented Japan at the FIFA Under-20 Women's World Cup in Costa Rica. Ishikawa was in the side that lost 3-1 against Spain in the final.

Twelve months later she was named in the 23-player Japanese squad for the Women's World Cup in Australia. Japan reached the quarter-finals before losing to Sweden.

Momiki, a striker born in New York, is the most experienced of the trio and has had WSL experience with Leicester City.

She started her career in Japan with Nippon TV Beliza before returning to the States to join Seattle-based OL Reign. She then had a couple of seasons on loan in Sweden with Linkoping before making the move permanent.

Her next port of call was England when she joined Leicester City in 2024.

On the international stage, Momiki represented Japan at every youth level and was closing in on 50 full caps when she came to Everton. She played

Rion Ishikawa

Hikaru Kitagawa

stories. It made me really proud knowing I will be a part of the Club's history, so I can't wait."

Kitagawa was also delighted to be linking up with her compatriots.

"I decided to join this team because I watched them last season and spoke to the head coach," she said. "It is a new start for the girls to use this stadium and I'm really happy to come here and play with them."

As for Ishikawa, she sees the move to Everton as a major step in her career progression at both club and international level: "I believe this league is the best in the world. I am really lucky I can compete in it. I will work hard to achieve the best possible results with my teammates. I will be able to challenge myself with high intensity every day, and by doing so, I will be able to perform better at the World Cup and the Olympics."

in the 2019 Women's World Cup, the 2024 Olympic Games and the 2025 SheBelieves Cup.

The SheBelieves Cup is a high-profile invitational women's soccer tournament held in the United States, and in 2025 Japan won it for the first time. Australia, Colombia and USA were the other teams in the tournament, and Japan lifted the trophy by winning all three of their games. Momiki opened the scoring in the crucial last game win against USA.

Momiki said: "Women's football is growing so much. In England, and also at Everton, there is a clear goal to grow our game as much as possible. That ambition makes me even more excited and was a key reason for me coming here. I went on the guided tour of Goodison Park and I heard all of the

Yuka Momiki

GETTING TO KNOW
CHARLY ALCARAZ

His full name is Carlos Jonas Alcaraz Durán but he prefers to be known as Charly.

He was born in La Plata (Argentina) on 30 November 2002—David Moyes was the Everton manager at the time!

His first professional team was Racing Club, who play in the Argentine Primera Division, making his senior debut in January 2020 at the age of 17.

In 2022, Alcaraz scored the winning goal as Racing Club beat Boca Juniors in the Argentine Champions Trophy final. It was an incredible game—TEN players were sent-off and it had to end early as Boca only had six players left on the pitch! Alcaraz was one of the players red-carded!

In January 2023, he came to England to join Southampton.

He made his debut for Southampton in a 2-1 Premier League victory against... Everton!

That game was Frank Lampard's last one at Goodison Park as manager of Everton. Sean Dyche replaced him a couple of weeks later.

In January 2024, Alcaraz joined Serie A team Juventus on loan for the rest of the season, making 12 appearances.

He was an unused substitute when Juventus won the Copa Italia final against Atalanta. Former Blue Moise Kean was also on the bench for Juve, while Ademola Lookman was in the Atalanta side.

The following August, Alcaraz left Southampton for good when he signed a permanent deal with Brazilian club, Flamengo.

In January 2025, he came back to the Premier League to join Everton on loan.

He scored his first goal in a 2-1 win against Crystal Palace, netting the winner.

In May 2025, Alcaraz became the first Everton player since Tim Cahill to score away goal winners with his first two goals for the club... when his header secured a 1-0 victory at Newcastle United.

Alcaraz has represented Argentina at Under-23 level but has not yet won a senior cap, despite being called-up for a couple of international squads.

Alcaraz scored the very first Cup goal at Hill Dickinson Stadium when he opened the scoring against Mansfield Town in the Carabao Cup 2nd round.

LET'S MEET...

TYLER DIBLING

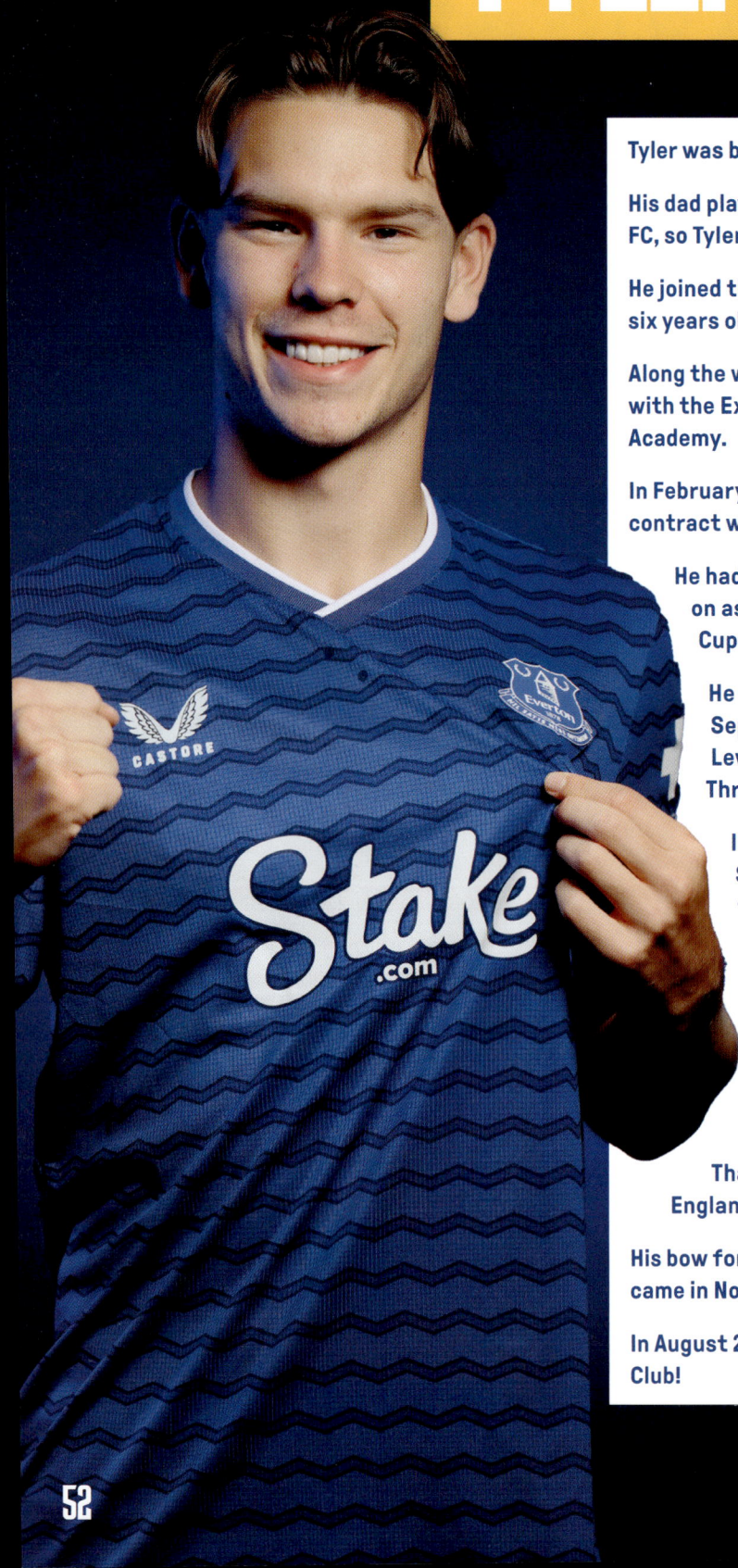

Tyler was born in Exeter on 17 February 2006.

His dad played for the local team, Axminster Town FC, so Tyler joined the same club as a junior.

He joined the Southampton Academy when he was six years old.

Along the way, a young Tyler also had a season with the Exeter City youth team and the Chelsea Academy.

In February 2023, he signed his first professional contract with Southampton.

He had already made his senior debut, coming on as a substitute for the Saints in a Carabao Cup tie against Gillingham.

He made his England Under-18 debut in September 2023 against France. Myles Lewis-Skelly (Arsenal) was also in the young Three Lions team that day.

In 2023/24, he was part of the Southampton squad that won promotion from the Championship to the Premier League, although he didn't feature in the Play-Off final at Wembley against Leeds United.

In September 2024, Tyler scored his first senior goal for the Saints in a 1-1 draw against Ipswich Town.

That same month, he made his debut for the England Under-19 team in a 2-2 draw with Italy.

His bow for Lee Carsley's England Under-21 team came in November 2024 in a 0-0 draw with Spain.

In August 2025, Tyler signed for Everton Football Club!

David Moyes has a proven track record of developing young players. How influential was he in your move to Everton?

I think the manager is perfect for me. Obviously, he's helped so many players before who were in my position, so I know he's going to be good for me. I hope he can get the best out of me and I'm sure he will. He said that I'm exciting and he wanted me to be part of the team. Hopefully he can make me play for England one day – they were his words!

You're still very young, but there's a chance for you to learn from the talent we have in this squad, like Jack Grealish and Iliman Ndiaye.

They're similar players to me, just with more experience, so I'm just going to take on board their advice every day and I'll get to watch them in training every day. I'm really excited to play with them. The signings we've brought in – like Jack Grealish – are massive, massive players. It's only going to make the Club better and hopefully we can get some silverware this year or a Europe finish.

What can Evertonians expect from Tyler Dibling?

I'd say the wow factor in my game is my dribbling. That's what I'm best at and that's what's going to excite the fans, and I hope I'll get to do a lot of it. I want to play as many games as I can and help the team as much as I can with goals and assists.

Tyler, how does it feel to be an Evertonian?

I'm buzzing! It took so long, and I felt Everton already, even when I wasn't even in the building, just from social media and from people telling me about the Club. I think it's the perfect match with the project that the Club is on right now, with the new stadium. The fans here are unreal, so that's a big plus, and it has a family feel to it. It was a no-brainer, really. I think I've come at the perfect time and hopefully I can be here for many years.

You played in the last ever Premier League game at Goodison Park for Southampton in May 2025. What was that like?

When we walked out at Goodison it was mental, it was so loud! I was looking around and thinking, 'This is quality', and I didn't know I'd be coming to Everton at that time but that was a really good insight for me into what it's like here with the fans and the atmosphere they can create. There's no better feeling than when you're doing well in football and to feel that love from the fans. It's one of the best feelings ever and I'm excited to play here.

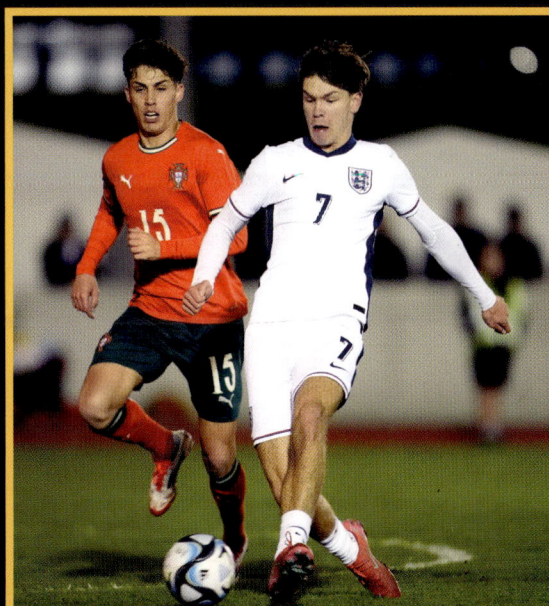

MATCH THE NAMES!

You'll probably need the help of a grown-up with this quiz.
Here are ten Everton players and all you have to do is pair
together the ones with the same surname!

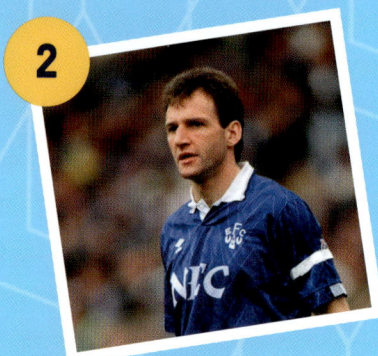

1

2

3

4

5

6

7

8

9

10

ANSWERS
ON PAGES
62-63

WORDSEARCH

See how long it takes you to find all the Everton England internationals in this grid...

A	D	X	F	P	X	Y	Y	I	J	T	B	Z	T	M	M	S	F	N	W
O	N	D	A	Q	B	E	G	E	V	K	Q	K	L	L	A	B	K	R	U
B	K	R	Y	V	N	G	J	F	L	Q	N	O	H	U	X	X	M	L	A
E	B	S	W	O	W	E	N	A	E	K	A	T	H	Z	F	O	M	S	N
P	F	H	O	O	Z	X	G	Z	I	A	R	Q	Z	Y	U	F	V	S	P
A	W	R	S	D	P	X	L	O	E	V	E	A	G	O	X	J	H	K	E
U	Q	A	H	B	I	J	A	G	Z	Z	K	W	B	I	A	W	T	B	R
J	H	H	T	H	T	E	I	F	L	H	E	Z	K	G	N	E	N	O	L
G	S	A	J	A	H	T	R	Y	C	Y	N	P	I	N	X	Y	J	N	D
R	J	Y	K	Z	S	M	H	N	C	W	I	E	G	B	J	J	V	H	R
E	B	P	B	W	P	Z	X	K	C	C	L	B	N	X	K	W	J	U	O
W	H	Y	H	X	U	E	I	F	X	K	R	Y	E	G	E	I	C	C	F
E	P	G	M	T	O	U	Z	O	A	I	S	P	J	N	R	N	A	Z	K
R	I	N	Y	E	M	I	V	X	P	P	H	T	G	Z	R	F	U	S	C
D	S	F	R	C	P	E	J	L	R	V	J	C	V	X	J	E	F	E	I
H	U	H	E	Z	U	Q	N	W	E	B	A	I	N	E	S	Y	G	K	P
Y	F	I	T	H	L	I	A	M	U	C	K	O	Z	Z	J	J	P	U	O
Y	E	R	N	Z	Y	M	M	X	I	I	H	J	C	R	F	I	J	J	D
U	V	T	R	N	M	L	S	S	J	Z	I	Z	C	F	K	C	Q	N	T
I	J	N	B	X	S	P	O	J	K	S	T	H	U	T	V	W	G	R	M

JAGIELKA

ROONEY

BAINES

BALL

REID

LINEKER

KEANE

PICKFORD

BARKLEY

OSMAN

ANSWERS ON PAGES 62-63

55

MICHAEL KEANE

TELL THE FUTURE!

Think you can predict what's going to happen in the world of football in 2026? Guess who will win these top prizes and then when the season finishes, get your Annual off the shelf and see how you did! You could even challenge your friends to do the same and see who gets the most right!

COMPETITION	2024/25 WINNERS	2024/25 WINNERS
PREMIER LEAGUE	LIVERPOOL	
CHAMPIONSHIP	BURNLEY	
LEAGUE ONE	BIRMINGHAM CITY	
LEAGUE TWO	DONCASTER ROVERS	
NATIONAL LEAGUE	BARNET	
CHAMPIONS LEAGUE	PARIS ST GERMAIN	
EUROPA LEAGUE	TOTTENHAM HOTSPUR	
EUROPA CONFERENCE	CHELSEA	
FA CUP	CRYSTAL PALACE	
LEAGUE CUP	NEWCASTLE UNITED	
SCOTTISH PREMIER LEAGUE	CELTIC	
WOMEN'S SUPER LEAGUE	CHELSEA	
WOMEN'S FA CUP	CHELSEA	
EVERTON'S TOP SCORER	ILIMAN NDIAYE	
PREMIER LEAGUE TOP SCORER	MOHAMED SALAH	

TOTAL SCORE ..../15

EVERTON IN THE COMMUNITY

Everton in the Community provides a football pathway so that any disabled person can reach their full football potential depending on their desire and ability.

Its disability programme currently has 13 disabled teams that represent the Club. These teams vary from impairment specific, such as Down syndrome or amputee, to teams of specific age and gender.

Everton in the Community's PAN disability teams consist of people with different disabilities playing in the same team with a similar ability level. The teams train every week under the supervision of the hardworking and dedicated coaches and play in local, regional, national and sometimes international competition.

The projects give many benefits for disabled people including reducing social isolation, increasing vital social interaction and competitive opportunities.

Each year, the charity hosts the prestigious 'Disability Player of the Year Awards' where the Football Club celebrates the achievements of the disabled participants. Seamus Coleman attends this ceremony every year.

Since the disability programme inception, over 50 participants have gone on to play internationally and represent their country through European Championships, World Cups and at Paralympic level.

During the 2024/25 season, the wonderful players of the Down syndrome squad got the full 'first team treatment' when a game was screened 'live' on the Everton YouTube channel.

The match was part of the World Down Syndrome Day celebrations and took place at the EitC Cruyff Court pitch on Spellow Lane—no more than a Jordan Pickford goal-kick away from Goodison Park!

The Down syndrome squad was split into two teams that were managed by Club Ambassadors, and former players, Ian Snodin and Graham Stuart.

A couple of players from each team were interviewed 'live' in front of the camera before the game—just like they do it in the Premier League!

After delivering their respective team talks, Snods and Graham then joined regular first-team match commentator Darren Griffiths for the 'live' coverage of the game.

"It was absolutely brilliant!" said Snods afterwards. "We told the lads before the game that when they score a goal, they have to run up to the camera and do a special celebration—and they certainly did that! Their enthusiasm is just infectious and I love watching them play. They are so proud to be representing Everton Football Club, and quite rightly so. Once they put that royal blue jersey on, they are Everton players."

Snods and Graham are also regulars at the Awards evening.

"It's one of the highlights of the calendar year!" said Graham. "Myself and Snods go every year and we love to see the guys celebrating their achievements. There are always trophies and medals to present, and the success of the teams is a testament to the effort put in by the coaches. They are the unsung heroes."

STEVE JOHNSON

Steve Johnson is a three-time World Cup winning amputee footballer who is also the Equality, Diversity and Inclusion Officer for Everton in the Community.

He oversees the Club's disabled football programme and had a tremendous playing career himself, winning 130 international caps for the England Amputee football team and being named World Amputee Footballer of the Year in 1999.

Passionate about football from a young age, Steve continued to play after his leg was amputated following an accident at the age of 21, and he has led the disability programme at Everton in the Community since 2003 shaping the initiative into one of the most respected in Europe, providing football and physical activity opportunities for thousands of disabled children and adults each year.

GETTING TO KNOW

ADAM AZNOU

He started off with Bayern Munich II, who compete in the fourth tier of German club football.

In January 2024, Adam was named in Bayern's first-team squad for the very first time. He was an unused substitute in a Bundesliga match away at FC Augsburg.

In November of that year, he made his senior debut, coming off the bench to replace Canadian international Alphonso Davies, during a match against FC Union Berlin.

In February 2025, he was loaned to La Liga outfit Valladolid for the rest of the season.

In July 2025, Adam made the move to Everton!

In August 2024, he won his first senior international cap for Morocco, against Lesotho in an African Cup of Nations qualifier.

Adam is the first Moroccan international to sign for Everton!

Adam was born on 2 June 2006 in the Spanish city of Barcelona.

His first proper team was Club de Futbal Damm – a youth club set-up in his hometown.

In 2019 he moved upwards to the famous youth Academy at Barcelona.

He soon became a target for other big European clubs and in 2022 he switched to the academy of German giants, Bayern Munich.

Celebrating a Bayern goal with Eric Dier and Harry Kane

If Adam plays for Morocco in the 2025/26 African Cup of Nations, he will become the 9th Everton player to do so.

The previous ones are – Idrissa Gueye (Senegal), Alex Iwobi (Nigeria), Yanick Bolasie (Congo DR), Christian Atsu (Ghana), Yakubu (Nigeria), Joseph Yobo (Nigeria), Steven Pienaar (South Africa) and Henry Onyekuru, who played for Nigeria but never made a first-team appearance for Everton.

GETTING TO KNOW MERLIN RÖHL

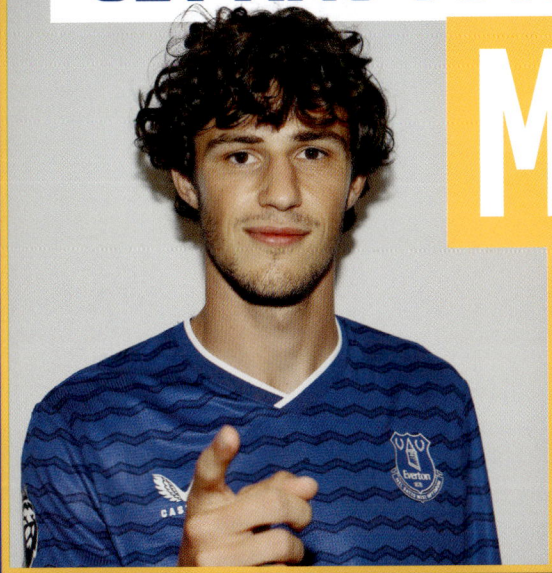

In the quarter-finals, Merlin scored the winning goal in extra-time against Italy. He netted in the 117th of a dramatic match that saw his team edge out the Italians 3-2.

He won 13 caps for Germany Under-21s, scoring three goals.

On 1 September, with time running out in the transfer window, Merlin signed for Everton!

Merlin was born in the German city of Potsdam on 5 July 2002.

As a youth footballer he came through the ranks at SV Babelsberg – a local team based on the outskirts of Berlin.

He made his senior football debut in November 2020 for FC Ingolstadt 04, who currently play in the third tier of German League football.

During Merlin's time there, he helped the team win promotion to the second tier.

At international level, Merlin has represented Germany at Under 18,19, 20 and 21 level.

In August 2022 he moved up to the Bundesliga with SC Freiburg.

He started off in their second team, who also play in the third tier, before progressing through to the first team.

In November 2023, he scored his first Bundesliga goal away at RB Leipzig.

In the summer of 2025, Merlin was part of the Germany Under-21 squad that reached the final of the European Championships.

They lost to England in the final, with Merlin coming off the bench for the Germans in the 80th minute.

WHAT THEY SAID...

"He's got pace, great movement. He can be a real difference-maker."
FORMER FREIBURG HEAD COACH CHRISTIAN STREICH

"He fought his way into [Freiburg's] team. That's not easy. He focused on defensive work and also came into his own offensively. He's very quick and determined. He's very dangerous."
GERMANY U21 HEAD COACH ANTONIO DI SALVO

"The Everton fans are passionate and demand hard work and that's what I like as it matches what I can bring. I see myself as a box-to-box midfielder and I feel I can bring my qualities to this team after having discussions with the manager. I think versatility is a strength of mine and the style of my game will suit the Premier League."
MERLIN RÖHL AFTER JOINING THE BLUES

QUIZ ANSWERS

PAGE 7
1. Celtic
2. Centre-half
3. Manchester United
4. Frank Lampard
5. Tottenham Hotspur
6. Fulham, Southampton, Newcastle United

PAGE 12
1. Cole Palmer
2. Nottingham Forest and Bournemouth
3. Peterborough United
4. Bournemouth
5. Newcastle United
6. Ollie Watkins
7. Iliman Ndiaye
8. Wolves and Leicester
9. Leicester City, Ipswich Town, Southampton
10. David Raya and Matz Sels
11. Leeds United, Burnley and Sunderland
12. Paris St Germain and Inter Milan
13. 5-0 for PSG
14. Manchester United and Tottenham Hotspur
15. Sevilla

PAGE 17
1. Gabriel Martinelli (Arsenal)
2. Brennan Johnson (Tottenham Hotspur)
3. Dan Burn (Newcastle United)
4. Jarrad Bowen (West Ham)
5. Moises Caicedo (Chelsea)
6. Jeremy Doku (Manchester City)
7. Chris Wood (Nottingham Forest)
8. Dean Henderson (Crystal Palace)
9. Antoine Semenyo (Bournemouth)
10. Kaoru Mitoma (Brighton)

PAGE 24-25
1. Marcus Bent
2. Gareth Barry and Joleon Lescott
3. Anders Limpar
4. Michael Ball
5. Duncan Ferguson
6. Sylvain Distin
7. Francis Jeffers
8. Bob Latchford
9. Steven Naismith
10. Leon Osman
11. Paul Rideout
12. Tomasz Radzinski
13. Joe Parkinson
14. Tony Cottee and Stuart McCall
15. Dave Jones

PAGE 28
1. Ben Godfrey
2. Andres Gomes
3. Alex Iwobi
4. Samuel Eto'o
5. Andros Townsend
6. Conor Coady
7. Ellis Simms
8. Josh King
9. Morgan Schneiderlin
10. James Rodriguez

PAGE 38
1. Seamus Coleman
2. Iliman Ndiaye
3. Dwight McNeil
4. James Tarkowski
5. Charly Alcaraz
6. James Garner
7. Idrissa Gana Gueye
8. Vitalii Mykolenko
9. Jordan Pickford
10. Michael Keane